The Sto
of
RANGERS

JACK GEDDES

Special thanks to:

Derek Lowe for reading it, living it and loving it!

Foreword

Over the years, millions of fans have followed Rangers and they all have their favourite goals, players and games.

The history of our great Club has been told many times – but now for the first time the story of how Rangers became the most successful football team in the world has been written for our young supporters.

Young Teddy Bears everywhere will love discovering what has made us Simply The Best and I hope they enjoy *The Story of Rangers* as much as I did.

John Greig

Dedication

In memory of Henry Law, thanks grandpa.

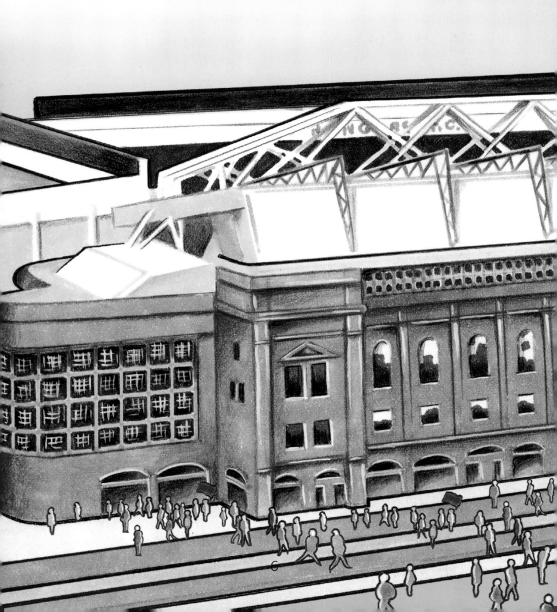

Rangers are the most successful football club in the world.

They have won more than 100 trophies, which is a world record.

More than 50 of these trophies have been league championships. This, too, is a world record.

Rangers are famous wherever football is played, and play their home games in a wonderful stadium in front of 50,000 fans. Yet when they started out, over 130 years ago, they didn't have a pitch of their own. In fact, they couldn't even afford to buy a kit or a ball!

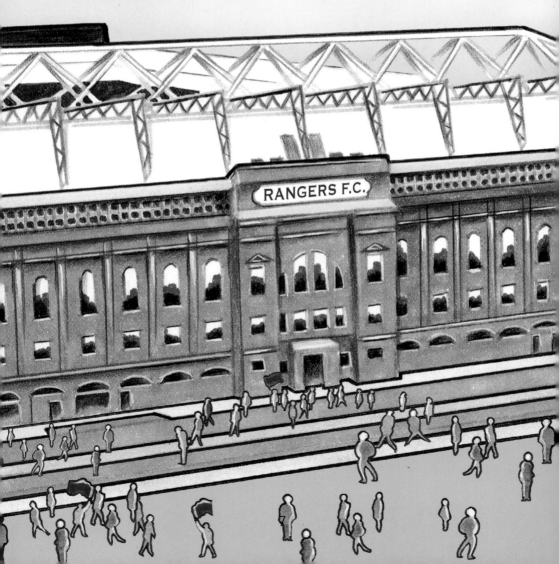

Four friends – brothers Moses and Peter McNeil, Peter Campbell and William McBeath – decided to start a football team. Moses suggested Rangers as a name for the new club as he had heard of an English rugby team with that name. His pals liked it.

So the new club had a name, but it still did not have a ground, or a strip, or a ball.

The first home game was played at Glasgow Green, not far from where Celtic Park now stands.

Moses, Peter and the other 'Rangers' had to make sure they arrived early to claim the pitch.

Most players wore ordinary clothes, and the ball was second hand. Rangers drew their first ever match 0–0 against a team called Callander FC.

By the time they played their second match, Rangers had managed to find a proper kit. Wearing the famous Light Blue for the first time, they beat Clyde 11–0.

William Wilton became the first Rangers boss in 1889.

William was a strict man, and liked his players to dress smartly – a tradition that remains strong at Rangers to this day.

The next year the 12 major clubs in Scotland decided to start a league and at the end of the season Rangers and Dumbarton were joint champions.

It was the first of many celebrations.

William also led his team to their first Scottish Cup win in 1894 and he was manager when they set a world record that has never been equalled. Rangers are the only team ever to win all their league games in a season. It was 1898–99 and Rangers took full points from all 18 matches.

1899 LEAGUE TABLE

Scottish Division One

	P	W	D	L	F	A	PTS
Rangers	18	18	0	0	79	18	36
Hearts	18	12	2	4	56	30	26
Celtic	18	11	2	5	51	33	24
Hibernian	18	10	3	5	42	43	23
St Mirren	18	8	4	6	46	32	20
Third Lanark	18	7	3	8	33	38	17
St Bernard's	18	4	4	10	30	37	12
Clyde	18	4	4	10	23	48	12
Partick Thistle	18	2	2	14	19	58	6
Dundee	18	1	2	15	23	65	4

Later that year Rangers moved to Ibrox, where the present stadium now stands.

In 1920 William drowned in a boating accident. His assistant, Bill Struth, took over …

Bill was to be the most successful manager in Rangers' history. He was in charge for 34 years and had many great players.

The finest of them all was probably his first signing.

Alan Morton was bought from Queen's Park in 1920. He was a left-winger and was the most exciting player in the country. His nickname was the Wee Blue Devil because he tormented the other teams' defences. Alan played for Rangers for 13 years but his most memorable year was 1928.

In March he played for Scotland when they thrashed England 5–1. That team is remembered to this day as the Wembley Wizards.

Then, in May, Alan lined up in the Scottish Cup final against Celtic, in front of a huge crowd of 118,000.

Rangers had not lifted the Cup for 25 years and were desperate to win.

In the first half Celtic were on top and the Rangers goalkeeper Tom Hamilton made some great saves, but in the second half it was a different story. Captain Davie Meiklejohn scored a penalty and Rangers went on to record a famous 4–0 victory.

Just one week later the Light Blues won the league championship again to complete the Club's first ever league and cup double.

OLD FIRM

Rangers and Celtic have been known as the Old Firm for more than 100 years. People realised that the clubs were making lots of money from their fans' rivalry. Whenever they played each other huge crowds would pay to watch – so despite being big rivals they were also business partners. Newspaper cartoon strips would show club bosses carrying big bags of money to the bank after a match. The Old Firm derby is one of the most famous games in the world.

Rangers won an incredible 15 out of 20 championships between 1920 and 1939. In that time there were wonderful players such as Davie Meiklejohn, Jerry Dawson, Alan Morton, Bob McPhail, Sandy Archibald and Andy Cunningham.

There was also a fantastic centre forward who still holds the Rangers record for most league goals scored in a season. His name was Sam English.

Sam was also involved in one of the most tragic accidents ever to happen on a football pitch. In September 1931 Celtic's goalkeeper, John Thomson, dived at Sam's feet in the penalty box. John's head collided with Sam's knee and he was carried off the pitch and taken to hospital, where he died. It was an accident and even John's family told Sam not to blame himself. However, Sam did not enjoy playing football as much again and he left Rangers only two years later.

It was a very sad end to what could have been a great career but Sam's 44 league goals that season still stand as a Rangers record.

When the Second World War started in 1939 many men had to go off and fight so official football competitions stopped.

Matches were still played as it was important that the people who were not fighting could still enjoy some normal activities. Throughout the war years Rangers won every unofficial league and even managed to record their biggest victory against Celtic, winning 8–1 in 1943.

In 1945 the war was won and a year later official football started again. Rangers had been the last champions before the war and were to become the first champions after it …

That same season a new competition started. It was called the League Cup and the Light Blues were the first team to win it, beating Aberdeen 4–0 in the final.

There was now a treble up for grabs each season. And Rangers were the first team to win that too!

By May 1949 they had already lifted both cups and were in second place in the championship. On a dramatic last day of the season, Dundee lost to Falkirk and Rangers beat Albion Rovers to ensure that they would go down in history once again.

TREBLE WINNING MANAGERS AND CAPTAINS

Season	Manager	Captain
1948–49	Bill Struth	Jock Shaw
1963–64	Scot Symon	Bobby Shearer
1975–76	Jock Wallace	John Greig
1977–78	Jock Wallace	John Greig
1992–93	Walter Smith	Richard Gough
1998–99	Dick Advocaat	Lorenzo Amoruso
2002–03	Alex McLeish	Barry Ferguson

THE IRON CURTAIN

After the Second World War, Europe was split between East and West. The dividing line became known as the Iron Curtain. Around the same time, Bill Struth was building a Rangers defensive line that most other teams could not break through.

It, too, was nicknamed the Iron Curtain.

The goalkeeper was Bobby Brown, with the two full backs, George Young and Jock Shaw, plus three half-backs – Ian McColl, Willie Woodburn and Sammy Cox. The Iron Curtain defence gave great confidence to their fellow players and fans. These men played hard, but fair, and they kept many clean sheets in one of the most successful Ibrox teams.

In 1954 Bill Struth stepped down as manager and former player Scot Symon took over. During these years there were many fine players at Ibrox. George Young had moved from right-back to become a great centre-half and a great captain.

Bobby Shearer and Eric Caldow were brilliant full-backs. There were excellent midfielders and strikers too in Ian McMillan, Willie Henderson, Ralph Brand, Jimmy Millar and Davie Wilson.

There was also a young man called John Greig who would go on to become a Rangers legend.

However probably the most gifted player of the time was Jim Baxter …

In 1960 Rangers paid Raith Rovers a record £17,500 to sign Jim. Due to his build he was nicknamed Slim Jim and many people think he is the best player ever to have worn the Light Blue of Rangers.

Jim was a left-footed midfielder and some of his best performances were against Celtic. In fact, in the 18 Old Firm games he played in Rangers only lost twice!

In 1961 Rangers became the first Scottish club to reach the final of a European competition, the European Cup Winners' Cup, losing to Fiorentina of Italy. They came even closer in 1967 when they lost 1–0 in extra time in the final against Bayern Munich. These disappointments were nothing compared to the tragedy that was about to strike the Club …

There had already been a disaster at Ibrox in 1902. During a Scotland v England international match part of the terracing collapsed, killing 26 people and injuring more than 500.

It was hoped those horrific scenes would never be repeated.

But disaster struck Ibrox again on January 2,1971. As fans were leaving the ground after an Old Firm game, there was a huge crush on the stairs. Sixty-six Rangers fans were killed.

So that the 66 will never be forgotten, their names have been written underneath the statue of John Greig outside Ibrox Stadium.

In a very short space of time Rangers moved from the darkest day in their history to one of the brightest …

In 1972 Rangers won through to their third European Cup Winners' Cup final against Moscow Dynamo. The game was played in Barcelona's Nou Camp Stadium. The Light Blues raced to a 3–0 lead just after half time through goals by Colin Stein and Willie Johnston, who scored twice.

The Russians came back strongly and with three minutes to go they scored their second goal. Rangers held firm to secure a famous 3–2 victory.

BARCELONA BEARS

On May 24, 1972 Rangers won their first European trophy. The game was played in the Spanish city of Barcelona, so the team has become known as the Barcelona Bears.

The historic campaign began with a defeat of French team Rennes. In the second round they drew 6–6 with Sporting Lisbon from Portugal over two legs. The referee then ordered a penalty shoot-out which Rangers lost, but a Scottish journalist realised that the referee had made an astonishing mistake, and that Rangers should go through on the new 'away goals' rule. So the Light Blues marched on!

Next to fall were Torino of Italy and then the mighty Bayern Munich from Germany. Finally on that magical night in Barcelona, Rangers beat Moscow Dynamo from Russia.

Captain John Greig had said he would not shave until his team were knocked out of Europe that season. That is why in pictures of John with the cup he is sporting a beard which he quickly shaved afterwards!

The Barcelona Bears: Peter McCloy, Sandy Jardine, Willie Mathieson, John Greig, Derek Johnstone, Dave Smith, Tommy McLean, Alfie Conn, Colin Stein, Alex MacDonald and Willie Johnston.

After the glory in Barcelona, manager Willie Waddell took on a new job at the Club. He was given the task of rebuilding the stadium to make it one of the best and safest in the world. The job of manager then passed to Willie's assistant.

Jock Wallace took over in 1972. He liked his players to be superfit and used to take them to Gullane on the east coast of Scotland and make them run up and down the sand dunes until they were exhausted.

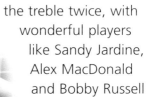

All the hard work soon paid off. In the famous 1973 Scottish Cup final against Celtic, Rangers won a classic game 3–2 with Tom Forsyth tapping in the winner on the goal line after Derek Johnstone had hit both posts with a powerful header.

The 1975 title triumph was Rangers first for 11 years and in the next three seasons they won the treble twice, with wonderful players like Sandy Jardine, Alex MacDonald and Bobby Russell all starring for Jock's team.

Despite this success Jock left and was replaced by John Greig. John was manager for five years before Jock came back for a second spell.

But by 1986 Rangers had not won the league for eight long years and the man in charge, David Holmes, decided something drastic had to be done.

Graeme Souness had won three European Cups with Liverpool and was one of the best and toughest midfielders in the world. He was only 32 and had no experience as a manager but Rangers took a huge gamble and named him player-boss. The gamble paid off and Graeme changed Scottish football forever.

NICKNAMES

Rangers *fans have given their heroes different nicknames over the years. The most obvious is* **The Gers** *which is just a shorter version of Rangers. This was then turned into* **The Bears**, *as it rhymed with Gers, and* **The Teddy Bears** – *which is also used to describe Rangers supporters.*

Due to the colour of the strips, fans are sometimes called **Bluenoses**. *In the early years Rangers were called* **The Royal Blues** *but are now usually called* **The Light Blues**.

Graeme's first recruit was Walter Smith, who became his assistant manager. Many think it was his greatest signing. Graeme then stunned British football by signing England captain Terry Butcher, one of the best centre-halfs in the world.

Within months Graeme lifted his first trophy when his team beat Celtic 2–1 in the League Cup final in October. The goals that day were scored by Ian Durrant and Davie Cooper.

Davie had been a great player for Rangers for nearly ten years, starting in the treble winning team of 1978.

Davie sadly died at the very young age of 39, but he will always be remembered fondly by those who filled Ibrox and loved to sing about 'Davie Cooper on the wing'.

Graeme's first league season ended in triumph, with Terry Butcher scoring a thumping header in a 1–1 draw against Aberdeen.

Rangers were champions again – and how the fans celebrated. Graeme stayed at Ibrox for five years and he turned Rangers into winners. In fact, they were champions in four out of five seasons.

Graeme brought many talented players to Ibrox. One of them, Maurice Johnston, was a former Celtic player.

Some Rangers fans were suspicious of him at first, but he soon won them over – especially when he scored against Celtic!

Graeme also helped arrange for his friend, David Murray, to buy Rangers in 1988. David's time as owner has been very successful.

In April 1991, Graeme left to join Liverpool and Walter Smith took over. A month later Aberdeen came to Ibrox needing just a draw to be champions. The stadium was packed and the atmosphere was electric. After a shaky start Rangers started to find their feet and five minutes before half-time Mark Hateley rose to bullet a header into the Aberdeen net.

Ten minutes after the break Mark scored again and Rangers had won their third championship in a row.

There was much more to come …

Walter's boys just kept winning, and winning.

They played some superb football and had great players like captain Richard Gough, Stuart McCall, John Brown and Paul Gascoigne.

Brian Laudrup was one of the most skilful players ever to wear the light blue. His most famous game was the 1996 Scottish Cup final when Rangers beat Hearts 5–1. Brian scored two and made the other three for Gordon Durie, who became the first Rangers player to score a hat-trick in a Scottish Cup final.

Andy Goram – nicknamed The Goalie – was the best keeper of his generation.

He saved Rangers many times with his skill and bravery, and kept 107 clean sheets in his 258 games.

The Goalie's performances in Old Firm games were so good that Celtic manager Tommy Burns said: 'On my gravestone they will write, "Andy Goram broke my heart"'.

While Andy was keeping goals out at one end, Rangers' greatest striker of all time was putting them in at the other. Ally McCoist had signed in 1983, and over the next 15 years he hit the back of the net 355 times for his beloved Light Blues.

He won nine championships, one Scottish Cup and a record nine League Cups. He was also the top-scoring player in Europe two seasons in a row in 1991–92 and 1992–93. He left and became a television star, but everyone knew he would return to Ibrox one day …

By season 1996–97, Rangers had won eight league titles in a row, and were desperate to equal Celtic's record of nine in a row.

They made a perfect start, winning their first seven games. In January at a packed Ibrox Rangers beat Celtic 3–1 with the help of a stunning free kick from German midfielder, Jorg 'The Hammer' Albertz.

By May '9 In a Row' was finally within touching distance. All Rangers had to do was beat Dundee United at Tannadice. It was a tough match, but Brian Laudrup scored with a flashing header to bring the league flag to Ibrox, and turn Walter's men into legends.

Walter and many of his players left the next year to make way for Rangers' first foreign manager …

Dick Advocaat came from Holland and set about rebuilding Rangers. He made clever signings in Arthur Numan, Gio van Bronckhorst and Stefan Klos. A young lad called Barry Ferguson had also broken into the team.

Dick's new team swept all before them, winning the two cups and also the 1999 championship by defeating Celtic 3–0 at Celtic Park.

The following season Rangers won the league by a record margin of 21 points and completed the double by beating Aberdeen 4–0 in the Scottish Cup final.

Off the pitch, Rangers built a fantastic training complex. It is called Murray Park after Rangers' chairman, David Murray, and is one of the best training grounds in Europe. Dick enjoyed his time at Ibrox but things were to change again …

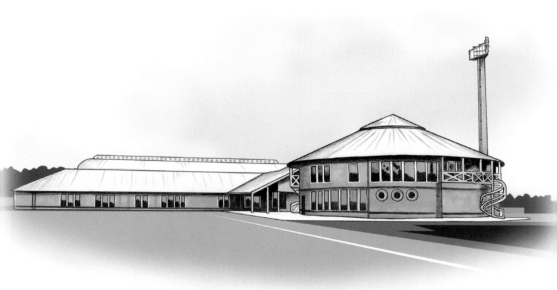

Alex McLeish became boss during the 2001–02 season and the following season led Rangers to a record seventh treble. In an incredible end to the league season a last-minute penalty against Dunfermline

50 LEAGUE CHAMPIONSHIPS

In season 2002–03 Rangers became the first team in world football to win 50 league championships.
In honour of this fantastic achievement Rangers now proudly wear five stars above their badge – one star for every ten titles.

made the score 6–1 and Rangers won the league by a single goal to become the first team ever to win 50 championships. People thought that this finish could never be repeated because it was so close.

But just two years later Rangers had to beat Hibs in the last league game and hope that Celtic would lose to Motherwell. Rangers won 1–0 at Easter Road but with only a few minutes left at Fir Park, Celtic were also winning 1–0. Then Motherwell scored two goals in the last few minutes. When they heard what was happening in Celtic's game the Rangers fans all over the world went wild.

The players were still on the pitch playing against Hibs, but they started to celebrate as well! Those last-minute goals also meant that the helicopter carrying the league trophy changed direction and instead of going to Motherwell headed for Edinburgh where Rangers were crowned champions again.

Alex won seven trophies at Ibrox before being replaced by French coach Paul Le Guen. Paul had a great record in France, but unfortunately his stay at Ibrox did not work out.

Rangers and their fans were now in need of a boost and it was to come from two of the most successful Rangers men of all time. Walter Smith gave up his job as Scotland coach to return as manager for the second time and Ally McCoist returned to Ibrox as assistant manager. Walter and Ally are now looking forward to leading the world's most successful football team to even more glory in years to come …